Jonathan Andrews

powerful 3-Minutes prayers for men

3-Minute Devotions for Men Encouraging Readings

Contents

1.

2.

3.

4.

5.

6.

7.

8.

9.

10.

11.

12.

13.

14.

15.

16.

17.

Introduction: The Power of 3-Minute Prayers for Men

In the rush of our modern lives, amidst the clamor of deadlines and responsibilities, it's easy for men to lose touch with the spiritual core that resides within us all. The demands of work, family, and the relentless ticking of the clock can leave us feeling spiritually parched, disconnected from the divine, and yearning for a deeper connection with our Creator. It's in these moments of longing that the practice of prayer and meditation becomes a lifeline, a source of solace and strength, and a pathway back to the wellspring of our faith.

For far too long, the notion of prayer and meditation has been shrouded in an aura of mysticism and perceived as a practice reserved for the cloistered and the contemplative. However, I stand before you as a fellow traveler on the journey of life, someone who has experienced the transformative power of prayer firsthand, and someone who understands the unique challenges and pressures that men face in the modern world. I'm not a guru or a sage; I am a brother on the same path, offering my hand in solidarity and sharing the profound insights I've gained through my own spiritual odyssey.

In "3-Minute Prayers for Men," we embark on a sacred journey together, one that invites you, the reader, to step out of the hustle and bustle of daily life, if only for a few precious minutes each day, and into the quiet sanctuary of your own heart. This book is a guide, a companion, and a source of inspiration for men seeking to nurture their spirituality, deepen their connection with God, and find solace in the midst of chaos. It is an invitation to rediscover the beauty of prayer and meditation as simple, accessible practices that can be seamlessly integrated into the fabric of your daily routine.

The 3-Minute Promise

You may wonder, why three minutes? In a world that celebrates the virtues of speed and efficiency, it might seem counterintuitive to allot such a brief period to something as profound as prayer and meditation. But here's the secret: three minutes is all you need to begin experiencing the profound effects of a regular prayer practice.

In these three minutes, we'll explore the power of concentrated intention, the potency of focused thought, and the beauty of quiet communion. These moments of prayer may occur during your morning commute, a quiet break at work, or as you sit in the stillness of your home. They are moments that can become the anchors of your day, the refuges where you find peace, strength, and inspiration.

Consider this: three minutes of sincere, heartfelt prayer can yield a lifetime of spiritual growth and transformation. Just as a tiny seed, when nurtured with care, can grow into a mighty oak, so too can these three-minute intervals of prayer and meditation become the foundation upon which you build a life deeply rooted in faith and love.

Meditation Tips for Men

Before we dive into the chapters that follow, let me offer you some practical meditation tips, tailored specifically for men:

Create a Sacred Space: Find a quiet corner in your home or workplace where you can retreat for your three-minute prayer sessions. This space, no matter how small, can be your sanctuary, a place where you can connect with the divine.

Set a Regular Time: Consistency is key. Choose a specific time each day for your three-minute prayers. It might be the moment you wake up, during your lunch break, or before bedtime. Establishing a routine will help make this practice a natural part of your day.

Breathe Deeply: As you begin your prayer and meditation, take a few deep breaths. This simple act helps calm the mind and body, making it easier to enter into a state of peaceful reflection.

Start with Scripture: Begin your meditation by reading a scripture passage or verse. The Bible is a wellspring of wisdom and inspiration. Allow the words to penetrate your heart and mind, and contemplate their meaning in the context of your life.

Visualize Peace: Close your eyes and visualize a peaceful scene. It could be a serene garden, a tranquil beach, or a sacred space from your own life. This visualization can help anchor your mind and create a sense of calm.

Express Gratitude: Take a moment to express gratitude for the blessings in your life. Gratitude is a powerful emotion that can shift your perspective and open your heart to the divine.

Reflect and Listen: After your initial reading and moments of gratitude, sit in silence. This is a time for listening and reflection. Allow God to speak to your heart, and be receptive to any insights or inspirations that arise.

End with a Prayer: Conclude your three minutes with a simple prayer. It could be a prayer of thanks, a request for guidance, or an expression of your love for God. Let your heart guide your words.

Scripture References for Meditation

Throughout this book, we will draw upon the rich tapestry of scripture to guide and inspire our prayers and meditations. Here are a few key passages to contemplate as you embark on this journey:

Psalm 46:10: "Be still, and know that I am God." This verse reminds us of the importance of quieting our minds and finding stillness in God's presence.

Philippians 4:6-7: "Do not be anxious about anything, but in every situation, by prayer and petition, with thanksgiving, present your requests to God. And the peace of God, which transcends all understanding, will guard your hearts and your minds in Christ Jesus." These verses offer comfort and assurance in times of anxiety.

Matthew 6:6: "But when you pray, go into your room, close the door and pray to your Father, who is unseen. Then your Father, who sees what is done in secret, will reward you." This verse emphasizes the power of private, heartfelt prayer.

Psalm 23: This beloved psalm reminds us of God's loving care and provision in our lives, even in the midst of challenges.

Meditation Quotes

To further enrich our meditation practice, we will also draw from the wisdom of spiritual thinkers and sages who have illuminated the path of prayer and contemplation. Here are a few meditation quotes to ponder as we journey together:

"Meditation is the tongue of the soul and the language of our spirit." — Jeremy Taylor

"In prayer, it is better to have a heart without words than words without a heart." — John Bunyan

"Prayer is not asking. It is a longing of the soul. It is daily admission of one's weakness. It is better in prayer to have a heart without words than words without a heart." — Mahatma Gandhi

"Prayer is not asking for what you think you lack, but for the abundance that you are." — Eckhart Tolle

As we embark on this transformative journey of prayer and meditation, remember that you are not alone. You are part of a community of men seeking a deeper connection with God, and together, we will explore the beauty of 3-Minute Prayers for Men. Let these moments of reflection and communion be a source of strength, healing, and inspiration as you navigate the currents of life.

In the chapters that follow, we will delve into the various facets of spirituality and meditation, each offering a unique perspective and opportunity for growth. Whether you are new to the practice of prayer or a seasoned traveler on this path, there is something here for you. So, let us begin this sacred journey together, with open hearts and a willingness to be transformed by the power of prayer.

May the words that follow guide you, inspire you, and lead you ever closer to the divine presence that resides within and around you. And may these three minutes of prayer become a source of light and strength in your life, illuminating the path to a deeper, more meaningful connection with God.

Chapter 1: Finding Solace in Daily Chaos

In the frenetic pace of our lives, as the world rushes around us, it's easy to feel like ships adrift on a turbulent sea. The demands of work, the responsibilities of family, and the incessant chatter of our digital devices can leave us feeling overwhelmed, disconnected, and spiritually thirsty. Yet, it is precisely in these moments of chaos and noise that the practice of prayer and meditation becomes an anchor for our souls, a lifeline that reconnects us to the tranquility and purpose we yearn for.

In this chapter, we will embark on a journey to find solace in the midst of daily chaos. We will explore how, in just three minutes, we can create pockets of peace that sustain us through the storm. Together, we will discover the transformative power of simple yet profound prayer and meditation practices that can be seamlessly woven into the fabric of our busy lives.

The Call to Stillness
 "Be still, and know that I am God." — Psalm 46:10

These words from the book of Psalms beckon us to a sacred pause, an invitation to step out of the whirlwind of our lives and into the calm center of our being. They remind us that, amidst the cacophony of the world, there exists a sanctuary of stillness where we can encounter the Divine.

In the hustle and bustle of our daily routines, we often neglect this call to stillness. We neglect to listen to the whispers of our hearts, the gentle nudges of our souls, and the loving presence of our Creator. Yet, it is in these moments of quiet reflection that we find the clarity, strength, and guidance we seek.

Three Minutes of Sanctuary

You might be wondering, how can three minutes make a difference? In the grand tapestry of our lives, three minutes can seem like a mere thread. However, within those three minutes, we can weave the fabric of our spirituality, creating a tapestry of presence and connection.

Imagine this scenario: you're at your desk, deadlines loom, emails pile up, and stress threatens to overwhelm you. In the midst of it all, you pause for just three minutes. You close your eyes, take a deep breath, and turn your attention inward. In those three minutes, you find solace. You reconnect with your inner sanctuary, where the chaos of the world cannot reach. You remember your purpose, your values, and the presence of the Divine that resides within you.

Meditation Tips for Men

Before we delve into a guided meditation, let's explore some practical tips that have helped men, like you and me, find solace in daily chaos:

The Power of Breath: Deep, conscious breathing is your anchor. Before you begin, take a few slow, deliberate breaths. Inhale deeply, feeling your chest rise, and exhale slowly, releasing tension. This simple act calms the mind and body, preparing you for the meditation ahead.

Scripture Reading: Start your meditation by reading a scripture passage that resonates with you. Psalm 23, as mentioned earlier, is a beautiful choice. Allow the words to wash over you, absorbing their meaning and wisdom.

Visualize Tranquility: Close your eyes and visualize a place of tranquility. It could be a serene forest, a mountaintop at dawn, or a peaceful chapel. Picture yourself there, absorbing the peace and stillness of that place.

Release Distractions: Acknowledge any distractions or worries that may arise during your meditation, but gently let them go. Imagine placing them in a basket and setting them aside. This is your time for solace and connection.

Attune to Your Heart: As you meditate, place your hand over your heart. Feel the rhythm of your heartbeat. This physical connection can help you stay grounded and connected to your inner self.

Guided Meditation: Finding Solace

Let's embark on a guided meditation together. Find a comfortable seat, close your eyes, and take a few deep breaths. Imagine yourself in a peaceful garden, surrounded by vibrant colors and the gentle rustling of leaves.

"The Lord is my shepherd; I shall not want. He makes me lie down in green pastures. He leads me beside still waters. He restores my soul." — Psalm 23:1-3

Picture yourself beside those still waters, feeling their coolness soothe your spirit. With each breath, you inhale the peace of this place, and with each exhale, you release tension and worry.

"Even though I walk through the valley of the shadow of death, I will fear no evil, for you are with me; your rod and your staff, they comfort me." — Psalm 23:4

As you meditate, imagine that you are walking through the valley of your daily challenges, but you are not alone. God is with you, guiding you with His loving presence.

"You prepare a table before me in the presence of my enemies; you anoint my head with oil; my cup overflows." — Psalm 23:5

Visualize a table set before you, a table of abundance and blessings. Your cup overflows with the goodness of life, and you are anointed with the oil of divine love and grace.

"Surely goodness and mercy shall follow me all the days of my life, and I shall dwell in the house of the Lord forever." — Psalm 23:6

As you conclude this meditation, feel the assurance that goodness and mercy are your constant companions. You are forever welcomed into the dwelling place of the Divine, where solace and peace await you.

Meditation Quotes

Let these meditation quotes resonate with you as you contemplate the practice of finding solace in daily chaos:

"In silence and stillness, you can hear the whispers of the Divine." — Unknown

"Peace. It does not mean to be in a place where there is no noise, trouble, or hard work. It means to be in the midst of those things and still be calm in your heart." — Unknown

"The greatest thing in the world is to know how to belong to oneself." — Michel de Montaigne

"Find a quiet spot amid life's chaos, and you will discover the wisdom of your own soul." — Unknown

As we conclude this chapter, remember that the practice of finding solace in daily chaos is not an escape from reality, but a return to your true self. In those three minutes of sanctuary, you reclaim your inner peace, reconnect with your purpose, and invite the Divine into your daily life. These moments are not a luxury; they are a necessity for your well-being, your spiritual growth, and your ability to navigate the challenges of this world with grace and resilience.

In the chapters that follow, we will explore more facets of Christian spirituality and meditation, each offering its own unique gift. But for now, embrace the power of three minutes, and let them be a source of solace and strength in your daily journey. May you find peace in the chaos, and may the stillness within you be a beacon of light guiding you home.

Chapter 2: The Strength of Faith

In the labyrinthine corridors of our lives, faith is the guiding torch that illuminates our path, dispelling the shadows of doubt and uncertainty. Faith is the cornerstone of Christian spirituality, the bedrock upon which we build our relationship with the Divine. In this chapter, we delve into the profound essence of faith—a force that empowers, sustains, and transforms us in the most extraordinary ways.

We will explore how faith serves as the bridge between the human and the divine, how it ignites the fires of hope even in the darkest of nights, and how it fuels our journey toward deeper spiritual connection. Together, we will learn how to trust in divine guidance, embrace God's plan for our lives, and conquer doubt and fear with unwavering faith.

The Bridge of Faith
"Now faith is the assurance of things hoped for, the conviction of things not seen." — Hebrews 11:1

These words from the book of Hebrews encapsulate the essence of faith—a belief in the unseen, an assurance in the midst of uncertainty. Faith bridges the gap between our human limitations and the infinite possibilities of the divine. It is the foundation upon which our spiritual lives are constructed.

For many, faith is not a single leap but a journey of steps, each step taken in trust and hope. It is a journey of gradually surrendering our doubts, fears, and ego-driven desires to a higher power. It is a surrender that ultimately leads to liberation—a liberation from the burdens of self-reliance and a journey toward the freedom of divine reliance.

Cultivating Trust in Divine Guidance

Faith, like a sturdy vessel, carries us across the tumultuous waters of life. But how do we cultivate and nurture this faith, especially in the face of life's storms? Let's explore some meditation tips that can help us trust in divine guidance:

Pray for Guidance: Begin your meditation with a simple prayer for guidance. Ask God to lead you, to illuminate your path, and to grant you the wisdom to discern His will.

Scriptural Reflection: Read and reflect upon scriptures that emphasize the importance of faith. Romans 10:17 reminds us, "So faith comes from hearing, and hearing through the word of Christ." Let these words permeate your heart.

Visualize Your Journey: Close your eyes and visualize your life's journey as a path. Picture yourself walking along this path, guided by a loving presence. As you take each step, trust that the path is unfolding as it should.

Release Control: Surrender your need for control during your meditation. Imagine releasing the reins of your life into the hands of God. Feel the weight of your burdens lifting as you relinquish control.

Express Gratitude: Express gratitude for the faith you have and for the guidance you've received in the past. Gratitude strengthens your trust and opens your heart to receive more.

Guided Meditation: Trusting in Divine Guidance

Let's embark on a guided meditation to deepen our trust in divine guidance. Find a quiet space, sit comfortably, and close your eyes. Take a few slow, deep breaths, and let go of tension.

"Trust in the Lord with all your heart and lean not on your own understanding; in all your ways submit to him, and he will make your paths straight." — Proverbs 3:5-6

Visualize yourself standing at a crossroads on your life's path. This crossroads represents a moment of decision, a moment where you seek divine guidance. You are not alone; God is with you.

"The steps of a good man are ordered by the Lord, and He delights in his way."
— Psalm 37:23

Imagine a soft, radiant light illuminating the path before you. This light represents God's guidance, His wisdom, and His presence. As you take a step forward, you feel the warmth of this light enveloping you, guiding you in the right direction.

"Commit to the Lord whatever you do, and he will establish your plans." — Proverbs 16:3

With each step, you surrender your decisions to the Divine. You release the need to control outcomes and trust that God's plan is unfolding. You feel a profound sense of peace and assurance.

"But when you ask, you must believe and not doubt, because the one who doubts is like a wave of the sea, blown and tossed by the wind." — James 1:6

As you conclude this meditation, you carry with you a deeper trust in divine guidance. You understand that faith is not the absence of doubt but the courage to move forward despite it. You know that, even in moments of uncertainty, you are supported by a loving presence.

Meditation Quotes

Let these meditation quotes serve as beacons of faith as you navigate your spiritual journey:

"Faith is taking the first step even when you don't see the whole staircase." — Martin Luther King Jr.

"Faith is the bird that feels the light and sings when the dawn is still dark." — Rabindranath Tagore

"Doubt your doubts before you doubt your faith." — Dieter F. Uchtdorf

"Faith is not the belief that God will do what you want. It is the belief that God will do what is right." — Max Lucado

As we conclude this chapter, remember that faith is not a destination but a lifelong journey. It is the bedrock of our spiritual lives, the strength that sustains us through trials, and the light that guides us in darkness. With unwavering faith, we embrace God's plan for our lives, trusting that He leads us toward our highest good. In the chapters ahead, we will explore more facets of Christian spirituality and meditation, each contributing to the deepening of our faith and the enrichment of our souls. May your faith continue to grow, and may it be a source of strength and inspiration on your path of spiritual discovery.

Chapter 3: Seeking Forgiveness and Redemption

In the tapestry of our lives, there are moments when we falter and stray from the path of righteousness. We carry the weight of our mistakes, our regrets, and our misdeeds, often allowing them to cast shadows on our spirits. But, in the realm of Christian spirituality, forgiveness and redemption shine as beacons of hope and grace. In this chapter, we will journey together through the profound landscape of seeking forgiveness and redemption, discovering the transformative power of God's love and mercy.

We will explore how, in just three minutes, we can open our hearts to the healing balm of forgiveness, release the burden of guilt and shame, and embrace God's unconditional love. Let us embark on this journey of redemption, understanding that no matter where we've been, we can always find our way back to the loving embrace of our Creator.

The Healing Power of Forgiveness

"If we confess our sins, he is faithful and just to forgive us our sins and to cleanse us from all unrighteousness." — 1 John 1:9

Forgiveness is a central theme in Christian spirituality—a divine act of love and compassion. It is a force that liberates us from the chains of our past, offering a fresh start and a new beginning. Forgiveness is not just an external act; it is an internal transformation, a healing of the soul.

When we seek forgiveness, we acknowledge our imperfections and lay bare our hearts before God. It is an act of vulnerability, a willingness to confront our own humanity. In return, we receive the gift of God's forgiveness—a forgiveness that cleanses, restores, and sets us free.

Releasing Guilt and Shame
"There is therefore now no condemnation for those who are in Christ Jesus." — Romans 8:1

Guilt and shame often shroud our souls like heavy fog, obscuring the light of God's love. These emotions can weigh us down, making us feel unworthy and distant from the divine. However, the truth of Christian spirituality is that, through Christ, we are freed from condemnation.

In our meditation practice, we can find solace and release from guilt and shame. Here are some tips to help you in this journey:

Confession and Repentance: Begin your meditation with a sincere confession of your sins. Pour out your heart to God, expressing remorse for your actions. Repentance is the first step towards forgiveness.

Scriptural Reflection: Meditate on scriptures that emphasize God's forgiveness. Psalm 103:12 reminds us, "As far as the east is from the west, so far has he removed our transgressions from us." Let these words soak into your soul.

Visualize Cleansing: Close your eyes and visualize a stream of pure, cleansing water. As you meditate, imagine stepping into this stream, allowing it to wash away the stains of guilt and shame. Feel the burden lifting as you emerge renewed.

Accept God's Love: During your meditation, focus on accepting God's love and grace. Imagine His unconditional love enveloping you, dispelling any doubts of your worthiness. Embrace His love as a warm, comforting embrace.

Release and Let Go: As you conclude your meditation, release your guilt and shame to God. Imagine placing these heavy burdens in His hands, trusting that He will bear them for you.

Guided Meditation: Embracing God's Forgiveness
Let's embark on a guided meditation to embrace God's forgiveness. Find a quiet space, sit comfortably, and close your eyes. Take a few deep breaths to center yourself.

"Create in me a clean heart, O God, and renew a right spirit within me." — Psalm 51:10

Imagine yourself standing in a vast, open field. In your hand, you hold a heavy sack filled with stones, each stone representing a mistake or sin you carry. These stones symbolize your guilt and shame.

"Come now, let us settle the matter. Though your sins are like scarlet, they shall be as white as snow." — Isaiah 1:18

In the distance, you see a brilliant light, radiating love and forgiveness. With each step towards this light, you feel the weight of your sack growing lighter. You understand that, in God's presence, forgiveness is not earned; it is freely given.

"I will sprinkle clean water on you, and you shall be clean from all your uncleannesses, and from all your idols I will cleanse you." — Ezekiel 36:25

As you reach the light, imagine setting down your sack of stones. A gentle rain begins to fall, cleansing you of your past. The rain represents God's forgiveness and grace, washing away every trace of guilt and shame.

"Therefore, if anyone is in Christ, he is a new creation. The old has passed away; behold, the new has come." — 2 Corinthians 5:17

As you conclude this meditation, know that you are a new creation, washed clean by God's forgiveness. You are free to walk forward in the light of His love, unburdened by your past mistakes.

Meditation Quotes
   Let these meditation quotes inspire your journey of seeking forgiveness and redemption:

"Forgiveness is the fragrance that the violet sheds on the heel that has crushed it." — Mark Twain

"To forgive is to set a prisoner free and discover that the prisoner was you." — Lewis B. Smedes

"The remedy for life's broken pieces is not classes, workshops, or books. Don't try to heal the broken pieces. Just forgive." — Iyanla Vanzant

"In faith, there is enough light for those who want to believe and enough shadows to blind those who don't." — Blaise Pascal

In this chapter, we have explored the transformative power of seeking forgiveness and redemption in Christian spirituality. We have learned that forgiveness is a divine gift, freely offered to us by a loving Creator. It is a gift that cleanses our souls, releases us from guilt and shame, and allows us to walk in the light of God's love. As we move forward on our spiritual journey, may we always remember that we are forgiven, that we are loved, and that we are free to embrace the   abundant   life   God   offers   us.

Chapter 4: Gratitude and Thanksgiving

In the tapestry of Christian spirituality, gratitude and thanksgiving are threads that weave a vibrant and harmonious pattern. The act of expressing gratitude opens our hearts to the abundant blessings that surround us, while the practice of thanksgiving is a way of acknowledging the divine source of those blessings. In this chapter, we will explore the profound significance of gratitude and thanksgiving in our spiritual journey and how they can transform our perspective on life.

We will delve into the practice of counting our blessings, celebrating life's simple joys, and giving thanks in all circumstances. As we navigate the intricacies of gratitude, we will discover that it is not just an act of politeness but a path to deeper spiritual fulfillment.

The Power of Gratitude

"Give thanks in all circumstances; for this is the will of God in Christ Jesus for you." — 1 Thessalonians 5:18

Gratitude is a disposition of the heart—a recognition of the goodness that permeates our lives. It is a recognition that our existence is filled with blessings, both big and small, and that these blessings are gifts from a loving Creator. Gratitude shifts our focus from what we lack to what we have, from what has gone wrong to what is right.

Gratitude is not reserved for moments of abundance and joy; it is equally vital during times of struggle and hardship. In fact, it is in the crucible of life's challenges that gratitude shines most brightly, for it reminds us that even in adversity, there is always something for which to be thankful.

Counting Your Blessings

"Bless the Lord, O my soul, and forget not all his benefits." — Psalm 103:2

The practice of counting your blessings is a powerful form of meditation in itself. It is an intentional act of reflecting on the goodness in your life. Let's explore some meditation tips to help you cultivate gratitude:

Begin Your Day with Thanks: As part of your morning routine, take a few moments to list things you are grateful for. These could be as simple as a new day, the warmth of sunlight, or the love of family.

Scriptural Reflection: Meditate on scriptures that emphasize thanksgiving. Colossians 3:17 reminds us, "And whatever you do, in word or deed, do everything in the name of the Lord Jesus, giving thanks to God the Father through him." Let these words guide your spirit.

Visualize Gratitude: During your meditation, visualize a garden of gratitude. Each flower in this garden represents a blessing in your life. As you focus on each flower, express your gratitude for that specific blessing.

Express Thankfulness: Throughout your day, take moments to express thanks silently or aloud. It could be as you enjoy a meal, witness a beautiful sunset, or experience a moment of joy. Share your gratitude with God.

Gratitude Journal: Consider keeping a gratitude journal. Each day, write down three things you are thankful for. This practice not only deepens your gratitude but also provides a record of your spiritual journey.

Guided Meditation: Celebrating Blessings

Let's embark on a guided meditation to celebrate the blessings in our lives. Find a quiet space, sit comfortably, and close your eyes. Take a few deep breaths to center yourself.

"I will give thanks to the Lord with my whole heart; I will recount all of your wonderful deeds." — Psalm 9:1

Imagine yourself in a serene garden bathed in golden light. This garden represents the abundance of blessings in your life. As you walk through this garden, notice the vibrant colors, the fragrant flowers, and the gentle breeze.

"The Lord is my shepherd; I shall not want." — Psalm 23:1

Visualize a banquet table in the center of the garden, covered with a feast of blessings. Each dish represents a unique blessing in your life. Take a moment to appreciate the variety and richness of these blessings.

"Oh give thanks to the Lord; call upon his name; make known his deeds among the peoples!" — 1 Chronicles 16:8

As you approach the table, choose one blessing that holds particular significance for you. Imagine savoring this blessing with gratitude, relishing the flavors and textures. As you do, express your thanks to God for this gift.

"The Lord has done great things for us; we are glad." — Psalm 126:3

After celebrating this blessing, move to another dish and repeat the process. Continue until you have acknowledged and celebrated several blessings. Feel your heart overflowing with gratitude.

"Rejoice always, pray without ceasing, give thanks in all circumstances; for this is the will of God in Christ Jesus for you." — 1 Thessalonians 5:16-18

As you conclude this meditation, remember that gratitude is not a one-time practice but a way of life. It is a continual offering of thanks to the Divine for the abundance of blessings that grace our existence.

Meditation Quotes

Let these meditation quotes inspire your practice of gratitude and thanksgiving:

"Gratitude unlocks the fullness of life. It turns what we have into enough, and more. It turns denial into acceptance, chaos to order, confusion to clarity. It can turn a meal into a feast, a house into a home, a stranger into a friend." — Melody Beattie

"Gratitude makes sense of our past, brings peace for today, and creates a vision for tomorrow." — Melody Beattie

"The thankful heart opens our eyes to a multitude of blessings that continually surround us." — James E. Faust

"Gratitude is not only the greatest of virtues but the parent of all others." — Marcus Tullius Cicero

In this chapter, we have journeyed through the transformative landscape of gratitude and thanksgiving. We have discovered that gratitude is not merely an expression of politeness but a profound spiritual practice that opens our hearts to the abundance of blessings in our lives. As we continue on our spiritual journey, may we cultivate gratitude as a daily habit, a habit that reminds us of the goodness that surrounds us and the divine source of all that we have. Gratitude is a bridge that connects us to God and to one another, a bridge that leads to a richer, more joyful, and more fulfilling life.

Chapter 5: Cultivating Compassion and Loving-Kindness

In the realm of Christian spirituality, compassion and loving-kindness are the radiant heartbeats that resonate with the teachings of Jesus Christ. These virtues are the embodiment of divine love—a love that extends not only to those who are close to us but also to strangers, adversaries, and even ourselves. In this chapter, we will embark on a journey to understand the transformative power of compassion and loving-kindness in our spiritual lives.

We will explore how, in just three minutes, we can cultivate a heart that is open, empathetic, and overflowing with love. As we delve into the depths of compassion and loving-kindness, we will discover that they are not only a response to the divine love we receive but also a pathway to experiencing the divine presence within and around us.

The Essence of Compassion

"Be kind and compassionate to one another, forgiving each other, just as in Christ God forgave you." — Ephesians 4:32

Compassion is more than just a feeling of sympathy or pity; it is a deep, empathetic response to the suffering of others. It is the recognition that we are all connected through our shared humanity and that, in moments of suffering, we have the capacity to alleviate each other's pain.

Compassion calls us to respond to suffering with kindness and love, just as God responds to our own suffering with boundless mercy and grace. It is a reflection of the divine love that dwells within us, waiting to be awakened and shared with the world.

The Power of Loving-Kindness

"The Lord is gracious and compassionate, slow to anger and rich in love." — Psalm 145:8

Loving-kindness, often referred to as "agape" love in Christian theology, is a love that transcends personal boundaries. It is a love that seeks the highest good of others, even at the expense of self. This love is characterized by its boundless generosity, forgiveness, and goodwill.

As we cultivate loving-kindness, we align ourselves with the very nature of God, who is the source of all love and kindness. Loving-kindness is not limited to our interactions with others but extends to how we treat ourselves as well. It is a love that recognizes our intrinsic worth and values the inherent dignity of every human being.

Cultivating Compassion and Loving-Kindness

Cultivating compassion and loving-kindness through meditation is a practice that can transform our hearts and minds. Here are some meditation tips to help you in this journey:

Begin with Self-Compassion: Start your meditation by extending compassion and loving-kindness to yourself. This is often the first step in cultivating these virtues for others. Offer yourself words of kindness and forgiveness.

Scriptural Reflection: Meditate on scriptures that emphasize compassion and loving-kindness. Colossians 3:12 encourages us to "clothe yourselves with compassion, kindness, humility, gentleness, and patience." Let these words guide your meditation.

Visualize Compassion: During your meditation, visualize a scene of suffering in the world. It could be a person in pain, a community facing hardship, or a global issue. As you meditate, imagine sending waves of compassion and loving-kindness to that situation.

Extend Compassion to Others: Gradually, expand your meditation to include others. Start with loved ones, then acquaintances, and eventually include those you may have conflicts with. Offer each person words of compassion and loving-kindness in your meditation.

Pray for a Compassionate Heart: Conclude your meditation by praying for a heart that is continually open to compassion and loving-kindness. Ask God to help you become an instrument of His love in the world.

Guided Meditation: Cultivating Compassion and Loving-Kindness
Let's embark on a guided meditation to cultivate compassion and loving-kindness. Find a quiet space, sit comfortably, and close your eyes. Take a few deep breaths to center yourself.

"But the fruit of the Spirit is love, joy, peace, forbearance, kindness, goodness, faithfulness, gentleness, and self-control." — Galatians 5:22-23

Imagine yourself in a serene garden, bathed in soft, golden light. This garden represents the garden of your heart, where compassion and loving-kindness grow. As you walk through this garden, notice the beauty of each flower and the gentle rustling of leaves.

"Love is patient, love is kind. It does not envy, it does not boast, it is not proud." — 1 Corinthians 13:4

Visualize a warm, radiant light emanating from your heart. This light symbolizes the love and kindness within you. With each breath, imagine this light growing brighter, expanding with love.

"But love your enemies, do good to them, and lend to them without expecting to get anything back. Then your reward will be great, and you will be children of the Most High, because he is kind to the ungrateful and wicked." — Luke 6:35

Think of someone you care deeply about, someone for whom you have great affection. Imagine sending waves of compassion and loving-kindness to this person. Visualize your love reaching them, surrounding them with warmth and care.

"Bless those who persecute you; bless and do not curse." — Romans 12:14

Now, bring to mind someone with whom you may have conflicts or difficulties. As you meditate, offer them words of compassion and loving-kindness. Visualize your love dissolving any barriers or animosity between you.

"May the God of hope fill you with all joy and peace as you trust in him, so that you may overflow with hope by the power of the Holy Spirit." — Romans 15:13

As you conclude this meditation, imagine the entire garden of your heart illuminated with the light of compassion and loving-kindness. Know that you carry this love with you, ready to share it with the world.

Meditation Quotes

Let these meditation quotes inspire your practice of cultivating compassion and loving-kindness:

"Let no one ever come to you without leaving better and happier. Be the living expression of God's kindness: kindness in your face, kindness in your eyes, kindness in your smile." — Mother Teresa

"Kindness is a language which the deaf can hear and the blind can see." — Mark Twain

"But love your enemies, and do good, and lend, expecting nothing in return, and your reward will be great, and you will be sons of the Most High, for he is kind to the ungrateful and the evil." — Luke 6:35

"Above all, keep loving one another earnestly, since love covers a multitude of sins." — 1 Peter 4:8

In this chapter, we have embarked on a journey to understand the transformative power of compassion and loving-kindness in our spiritual lives. We have discovered that these virtues are not merely feelings but intentional practices that can expand our hearts and bring us closer to the divine love that surrounds us. As we continue our spiritual journey, may we become vessels of compassion and loving-kindness, spreading God's love to all we encounter, and may our hearts be forever open to the beauty and potential for love in the world.

Chapter 6: Finding Inner Peace and Tranquility

In the chaotic orchestra of life, the search for inner peace and tranquility is a universal yearning that resonates deeply within the human spirit. It is a quest for a refuge of calm amidst the storms of existence, a sanctuary where we can reconnect with our true selves and the divine presence. In this chapter, we will embark on a profound exploration of inner peace—a treasure that can be discovered in as little as three minutes of meditation.

We will delve into the nature of inner peace, understanding that it is not the absence of external turmoil but a state of inner stillness and harmony. Through the practice of meditation, we will learn how to cultivate and nurture this peace, allowing it to become an abiding presence in our lives.

The Essence of Inner Peace
"Peace I leave with you; my peace I give to you. Not as the world gives do I give to you. Let not your hearts be troubled, neither let them be afraid." — John 14:27

Inner peace is a profound state of being that transcends the turbulence of the external world. It is a peace that dwells within, unaffected by the chaos that surrounds us. This peace is a gift from God, a reflection of His divine nature, and it is accessible to every seeker.

In our pursuit of inner peace, we come to realize that it is not dependent on external circumstances or the absence of challenges. Instead, it is a state of inner harmony that we can cultivate and carry with us, regardless of the storms of life.

Cultivating Inner Peace

Cultivating inner peace through meditation is a transformative practice that allows us to anchor ourselves in the present moment, releasing the burdens of the past and the anxieties of the future. Here are some meditation tips to help you in this journey:

Begin with Breath Awareness: Start your meditation by focusing on your breath. Pay attention to the rise and fall of your breath, the sensation of air entering and leaving your nostrils. Allow your breath to anchor you in the present moment.

Scriptural Reflection: Meditate on scriptures that emphasize inner peace. Philippians 4:7 reminds us, "And the peace of God, which surpasses all understanding, will guard your hearts and your minds in Christ Jesus." Let these words resonate in your heart.

Body Scan Meditation: During your meditation, perform a gentle body scan. Start at the top of your head and gradually move your attention down through your body, releasing tension and allowing each part to relax. This practice promotes physical and mental relaxation.

Visualize a Peaceful Scene: Close your eyes and visualize a place of profound peace and tranquility. It could be a serene beach, a tranquil forest, or a quiet chapel. Imagine yourself there, absorbing the peace of the surroundings.

Silence the Mind: As you meditate, you may notice thoughts and distractions arising. Instead of resisting them, acknowledge them without judgment and gently bring your focus back to your breath or your chosen point of meditation. Over time, this practice will quiet the mind.

Guided Meditation: Discovering Inner Peace

Let's embark on a guided meditation to discover inner peace. Find a quiet space, sit comfortably, and close your eyes. Take a few deep breaths to center yourself.

"Be still, and know that I am God." — Psalm 46:10

Imagine yourself in a tranquil garden, bathed in a soft, golden light. This garden represents the sanctuary of inner peace. As you walk through the garden, notice the gentle rustling of leaves, the soothing sound of a nearby stream, and the warmth of the sunlight on your skin.

"In peace I will both lie down and sleep; for you alone, O Lord, make me dwell in safety." — Psalm 4:8

Find a comfortable spot in the garden and sit down. As you close your eyes, turn your attention inward. Take a deep breath in, and as you exhale, imagine releasing any tension or worry. Feel the peaceful presence of God surrounding you.

"You keep him in perfect peace whose mind is stayed on you because he trusts in you." — Isaiah 26:3

Visualize a deep well of peace within your heart. This well is a source of endless tranquility, a place where you can always find refuge. Imagine yourself drawing from this well, filling your entire being with a profound sense of peace.

"Peace I leave with you; my peace I give to you. Not as the world gives do I give to you. Let not your hearts be troubled, neither let them be afraid." — John 14:27

As you continue to breathe deeply, allow the peace within you to expand, filling every corner of your body and mind. Let go of any worries or distractions, surrendering them to the divine presence.

"The Lord gives strength to his people; the Lord blesses his people with peace." — Psalm 29:11

As you conclude this meditation, carry with you the awareness that inner peace is not a distant destination but a present reality. It is a state of being that you can access at any moment, a peace that transcends circumstances and endures through all seasons of life.

Meditation Quotes

Let these meditation quotes inspire your practice of finding inner peace and tranquility:

"Peace is not the absence of trouble, but the presence of Christ." — Sheila Walsh

"Peace is the result of retraining your mind to process life as it is, rather than as you think it should be." — Wayne W. Dyer

"The peace of God is not the absence of fear. It, in fact, is His presence." — Tim Keller

"You will keep in perfect peace those whose minds are steadfast because they trust in you." — Isaiah 26:3

In this chapter, we have embarked on a profound journey to discover inner peace and tranquility—a treasure that resides within us, waiting to be unearthed through meditation and contemplation. We have learned that inner peace is not a distant ideal but a present reality, a state of being that we can cultivate and carry with us on our spiritual journey. As we continue our exploration of Christian spirituality and meditation, may we find solace and serenity in the depths of our own hearts, and may we become vessels of peace, radiating the divine presence to the world around   us.

Chapter 7: Surrendering to Divine Guidance

In the labyrinth of our lives, there comes a moment when we realize the limitations of our own understanding and the need to surrender to a higher wisdom. Surrendering to divine guidance is a profound act of trust—an acknowledgment that God's plan is far greater than our own. It is an act of humility, recognizing that we are not the architects of our destiny, but rather co-creators with the Divine.

In this chapter, we will explore the transformative power of surrender in the context of Christian spirituality and meditation. We will delve into the essence of surrender, understanding that it is not passive resignation but an active alignment with God's will. Through the practice of meditation, we will learn how to let go of our own agendas and open ourselves to divine guidance.

The Nature of Surrender
"Trust in the Lord with all your heart, and do not lean on your own understanding." — Proverbs 3:5

Surrender is a paradoxical journey—an invitation to release our grip on control in order to gain true freedom. It is an act of faith, entrusting our lives into the hands of a loving Creator who knows our path even when we do not.

True surrender is not characterized by passivity or indifference but by a deep, abiding trust. It is a surrender that allows us to take action from a place of inner peace, knowing that we are guided by divine wisdom. It is a surrender that leads us to a life of purpose, authenticity, and alignment with God's plan.

The Practice of Surrender

The practice of surrender through meditation is a transformative process that allows us to let go of the burdens of worry, anxiety, and self-doubt. Here are some meditation tips to help you in this journey:

Start with Gratitude: Begin your meditation by expressing gratitude for the gift of surrender. Recognize that surrender is an act of trust and a source of peace. Offer a prayer of gratitude for God's guidance in your life.

Scriptural Reflection: Meditate on scriptures that emphasize surrender. Psalm 37:5 encourages us to "Commit your way to the Lord; trust in him, and he will act." Let these words sink into your heart as you meditate.

Letting Go Meditation: During your meditation, visualize a stream of water representing your worries, doubts, and fears. As you breathe deeply, imagine releasing these burdens into the stream, watching them flow away, carried by the current.

Centering Prayer: Practice centering prayer as a form of surrender. Choose a sacred word or phrase that represents your intention to surrender. As you meditate, gently return to this word whenever your mind wanders.

Listening Meditation: Dedicate a portion of your meditation to simply listening. Invite God's presence into your meditation and offer a silent prayer, asking for guidance and wisdom. Practice listening for the still, small voice within.

Guided Meditation: Surrendering to Divine Guidance

Let's embark on a guided meditation to surrender to divine guidance. Find a quiet space, sit comfortably, and close your eyes. Take a few deep breaths to center yourself.

"Your word is a lamp to my feet and a light to my path." — Psalm 119:105

Imagine yourself standing at a crossroads in a lush forest. Each path represents a different direction in your life—your hopes, dreams, and plans. You carry a lantern that emits a warm, gentle light.

"I am the light of the world. Whoever follows me will not walk in darkness but will have the light of life." — John 8:12

In this moment, you realize the limitations of your own understanding and the need for divine guidance. You surrender your lantern to God, trusting that His light will guide your way.

"Trust in the Lord with all your heart, and do not lean on your own understanding. In all your ways acknowledge him, and he will make straight your paths." — Proverbs 3:5-6

As you release the lantern, you notice it is gently lifted into the air, illuminating the path before you. You understand that this path is not one of your own making but a path of divine guidance, leading you towards God's purpose for your life.

"I have been crucified with Christ. It is no longer I who live, but Christ who lives in me. And the life I now live in the flesh I live by faith in the Son of God, who loved me and gave himself for me." — Galatians 2:20

As you follow this path, you feel a deep sense of peace and assurance. You know that you are not alone, for the presence of God guides your every step. You surrender your worries, doubts, and fears to Him, trusting that His wisdom surpasses your own.

"For I know the plans I have for you, declares the Lord, plans for welfare and not for evil, to give you a future and a hope." — Jeremiah 29:11

As you conclude this meditation, remember that surrender is an ongoing practice—a daily choice to align your will with God's will. Surrender is not the absence of action but the presence of trust. May you carry this trust with you on your journey, knowing that you are guided by a divine hand and that the path ahead is filled with purpose and hope.

Meditation Quotes

Let these meditation quotes inspire your practice of surrendering to divine guidance:

"Let go and let God." — Anonymous

"The more you become a woman of prayer, the more you will trust God, and the less you will need to control people and situations." — Joyce Meyer

"Commit your work to the Lord, and your plans will be established." — Proverbs 16:3

"Surrender to what is. Let go of what was. Have faith in what will be." — Sonia Ricotti

In this chapter, we have explored the profound practice of surrendering to divine guidance—a journey that leads us from self-reliance to trust in God's wisdom. We have learned that surrender is not a passive resignation but an active alignment with God's will, a trust that leads us to a life of purpose and authenticity. As we continue our exploration of Christian spirituality and meditation, may we embrace surrender as a source of strength, a path to inner peace, and a gateway to God's abundant guidance in our lives.

Chapter 8: Cultivating Forgiveness and Healing

In the tapestry of our lives, forgiveness and healing are threads that can mend even the most frayed and broken parts of our souls. Forgiveness is an act of grace—a gift we extend to others and ourselves. Healing is a process of restoration—a journey toward wholeness in mind, body, and spirit. In this chapter, we will explore the profound interplay of forgiveness and healing in the context of Christian spirituality and meditation.

We will delve into the essence of forgiveness, understanding that it is not an excuse for wrongdoing but a liberation of our own hearts from the chains of resentment and bitterness. We will explore the path of healing, recognizing that it is a journey that requires courage, self-compassion, and divine intervention. Through the practice of meditation, we will learn how to cultivate forgiveness and invite healing into our lives.

The Transformative Power of Forgiveness

"Forgive us our sins, as we have forgiven those who sin against us." — Matthew 6:12

Forgiveness is a virtue that transcends human understanding. It is a choice to release the grip of anger, resentment, and the desire for revenge. Forgiveness does not condone wrongdoing but frees the forgiver from the burden of carrying another's offense.

In the Christian tradition, forgiveness is grounded in the understanding that we have been forgiven by God. Just as God's grace extends to us, so too are we called to extend grace to others. Forgiveness is a reflection of divine love—a love that seeks reconciliation and healing.

The Journey of Healing
"He heals the brokenhearted and binds up their wounds." — Psalm 147:3

Healing is a multifaceted journey that encompasses physical, emotional, and spiritual restoration. It is not always an instantaneous process but often unfolds gradually over time. Healing requires vulnerability—a willingness to confront and address the wounds of the past.

As we seek healing, we turn to God as the Divine Physician, the source of all healing and restoration. We recognize that God's love is a healing balm for our brokenness, and we trust in His timing and wisdom as we navigate the path toward wholeness.

Cultivating Forgiveness and Healing
Cultivating forgiveness and healing through meditation is a transformative process that can lead to emotional and spiritual liberation. Here are some meditation tips to help you in this journey:

Begin with Self-Forgiveness: Start your meditation by extending forgiveness to yourself. Acknowledge any self-criticism, guilt, or shame you may be carrying. Offer yourself words of self-compassion and forgiveness.

Scriptural Reflection: Meditate on scriptures that emphasize forgiveness and healing. Psalm 32:5 reminds us, "Then I acknowledged my sin to you and did not cover up my iniquity. I said, 'I will confess my transgressions to the Lord.' And you forgave the guilt of my sin." Let these words guide your meditation.

Loving-Kindness Meditation: Practice loving-kindness meditation, extending forgiveness and healing to others. Begin with loved ones, then gradually include those you may have conflicts with or resentments toward. Visualize their well-being and offer them forgiveness and healing.

Journaling: Consider keeping a forgiveness journal. Write down your reflections on forgiveness and healing, including any insights, emotions, or prayers that arise during your meditation practice.

Prayer for Healing: Dedicate a portion of your meditation to praying for healing in specific areas of your life or for those in need of healing. Surrender your wounds and burdens to God, trusting in His ability to bring restoration.

Guided Meditation: Embracing Forgiveness and Healing

Let's embark on a guided meditation to embrace forgiveness and healing. Find a quiet space, sit comfortably, and close your eyes. Take a few deep breaths to center yourself.

"Create in me a clean heart, O God, and renew a right spirit within me." — Psalm 51:10

Imagine yourself in a tranquil garden, bathed in soft, healing light. This garden represents the sanctuary of forgiveness and healing. As you walk through the garden, notice the gentle rustling of leaves, the soothing sound of a nearby stream, and the warmth of the sunlight on your skin.

"If we confess our sins, he is faithful and just to forgive us our sins and to cleanse us from all unrighteousness." — 1 John 1:9

Find a quiet, peaceful spot in the garden and sit down. As you close your eyes, turn your attention inward. Take a deep breath in, and as you exhale, imagine releasing any resentment, anger, or bitterness. Feel the healing presence of God surrounding you.

"Bear with each other and forgive one another if any of you has a grievance against someone. Forgive as the Lord forgave you." — Colossians 3:13

Visualize a gentle, cleansing rain falling from the heavens. This rain represents God's forgiveness and healing grace. Imagine it washing over you, cleansing your heart and soul of any wounds or grievances.

"He sent out his word and healed them, and delivered them from their destruction." — Psalm 107:20

As you meditate, bring to mind any person or situation for which you need to extend forgiveness. Visualize releasing them from the burden of your resentment, letting go of the chains that have bound your heart.

"And the peace of God, which transcends all understanding, will guard your hearts and your minds in Christ Jesus." — Philippians 4:7

As you conclude this meditation, remember that forgiveness and healing are ongoing processes. They require patience, compassion, and a willingness to surrender to God's transformative work. Trust in the power of forgiveness to liberate your heart and the healing grace of God to restore your spirit.

Meditation Quotes
    Let these meditation quotes inspire your practice of cultivating forgiveness and healing:

"To forgive is to set a prisoner free and discover that the prisoner was you." — Lewis B. Smedes

"The practice of forgiveness is our most important contribution to the healing of the world." — Marianne Williamson

"He himself bore our sins in his body on the tree, that we might die to sin and live to righteousness. By his wounds you have been healed." — 1 Peter 2:24

"Forgiveness is not an occasional act; it is a constant attitude." — Martin Luther King Jr.

In this chapter, we have explored the profound interplay of forgiveness and healing in the context of Christian spirituality and meditation. We have learned that forgiveness is a gift of grace that liberates our hearts, and healing is a journey toward wholeness in mind, body, and spirit. As we continue our exploration of Christian spirituality, may we embrace forgiveness as a path to freedom and healing as a journey toward wholeness, and may we extend these gifts to ourselves and others with compassion and grace.

Chapter 9: The Transformative Power of Gratitude

In the tapestry of our spiritual journey, gratitude is the vibrant thread that weaves together the moments of our lives into a tapestry of joy and contentment. It is a profound acknowledgment of the blessings that surround us, an appreciation of the divine gifts bestowed upon us each day. In this chapter, we will explore the transformative power of gratitude in the context of Christian spirituality and meditation.

We will delve into the essence of gratitude, understanding that it is not merely a polite expression of thanks but a way of life—an attitude that can shape our perception of the world. Through the practice of meditation, we will learn how to cultivate gratitude as a daily habit, a habit that leads to a richer, more joyful, and more fulfilling life.

The Essence of Gratitude

"Give thanks in all circumstances; for this is the will of God in Christ Jesus for you." — 1 Thessalonians 5:18

Gratitude is more than a polite response to blessings; it is a profound recognition of the goodness that surrounds us, both in moments of abundance and in times of challenge. It is an acknowledgment of the divine source of all that we have—a recognition that every breath, every moment, is a gift from God.

In the Christian tradition, gratitude is deeply intertwined with faith. It is an act of trust, believing that God's providence is at work in our lives. It is a response to the abundant grace and love that God pours out upon us daily.

The Practice of Gratitude

Cultivating gratitude through meditation is a transformative process that opens our hearts to the abundance of blessings in our lives. Here are some meditation tips to help you in this journey:

Begin with Breath and Awareness: Start your meditation by taking a few deep breaths to center yourself. As you breathe in, acknowledge the gift of life. As you exhale, release any tension or worry.

Scriptural Reflection: Meditate on scriptures that emphasize gratitude. Psalm 100:4 encourages us to "Enter his gates with thanksgiving, and his courts with praise! Give thanks to him; bless his name." Let these words guide your meditation.

Count Your Blessings: During your meditation, create a mental or written list of the blessings in your life. Reflect on both the significant and seemingly insignificant gifts, recognizing that every moment is an opportunity for gratitude.

Gratitude Journal: Consider keeping a gratitude journal where you regularly write down things you are thankful for. This practice can help you cultivate a habit of gratitude in your daily life.

Mindful Eating: If possible, practice mindful eating during your meditation. Savor each bite of food, recognizing the nourishment it provides and offering thanks for the abundance of sustenance.

Guided Meditation: Cultivating Gratitude

Let's embark on a guided meditation to cultivate gratitude. Find a quiet space, sit comfortably, and close your eyes. Take a few deep breaths to center yourself.

"Give thanks to the Lord, for he is good; his love endures forever." — Psalm 107:1

Imagine yourself in a serene garden, bathed in a soft, golden light. This garden represents the garden of your heart, where gratitude blossoms. As you walk

41

through this garden, notice the beauty of each flower, the vibrant colors, and the gentle rustling of leaves.

"Enter his gates with thanksgiving and his courts with praise; give thanks to him and praise his name." — Psalm 100:4

Visualize a warm, radiant light emanating from your heart. This light symbolizes gratitude—an ever-present source of joy and contentment. With each breath, imagine this light growing brighter, expanding with gratitude.

"Let the peace of Christ rule in your hearts, since as members of one body you were called to peace. And be thankful." — Colossians 3:15

Think of a specific blessing in your life—a moment of joy, a loving relationship, a personal achievement. As you meditate, express your gratitude for this blessing. Feel the warmth of thankfulness in your heart.

"Give thanks in all circumstances; for this is the will of God in Christ Jesus for you." — 1 Thessalonians 5:18

Now, expand your gratitude to encompass the broader tapestry of your life. Consider the various aspects of your life—your family

Chapter 10: The Sacred Practice of Compassion

In the tapestry of our spiritual journey, compassion is the golden thread that binds our hearts to the divine and to one another. It is a profound expression of love—an outpouring of empathy, kindness, and understanding toward all living beings. In this chapter, we will explore the sacred practice of compassion in the context of Christian spirituality and meditation.

We will delve into the essence of compassion, understanding that it is not merely a sentiment but a transformative force—a force that can heal wounds, bridge divides, and bring about profound inner and outer change. Through the practice of meditation, we will learn how to cultivate compassion as a way of life, a way that leads us to a deeper connection with God and a more compassionate world.

The Essence of Compassion

"Finally, all of you, have unity of mind, sympathy, brotherly love, a tender heart, and a humble mind." — 1 Peter 3:8

Compassion is more than a feeling of sympathy; it is an active response to the suffering of others. It is the embodiment of Christ's command to love our neighbors as ourselves. Compassion calls us to reach out, to listen, and to extend a helping hand to those in need.

In the Christian tradition, compassion is deeply rooted in the life and teachings of Jesus Christ. He exemplified compassion in his interactions with the marginalized, the sick, and the oppressed. His life serves as a model for us to follow in our own journeys of compassion.

The Practice of Compassion

Cultivating compassion through meditation is a transformative process that opens our hearts to the needs of others and deepens our connection with God. Here are some meditation tips to help you in this journey:

Begin with Loving-Kindness: Start your meditation by practicing loving-kindness meditation. Begin with extending love and compassion to yourself, then gradually include loved ones, acquaintances, and even those with whom you have conflicts.

Scriptural Reflection: Meditate on scriptures that emphasize compassion. Colossians 3:12 reminds us, "Put on then, as God's chosen ones, holy and beloved, compassionate hearts, kindness, humility, meekness, and patience." Let these words guide your meditation.

Compassion Visualization: During your meditation, visualize a world where compassion reigns. Imagine a world free from suffering, where love and empathy are abundant. Allow this vision to inspire your compassionate actions.

Breathing with Compassion: Practice a simple meditation where you inhale compassion and exhale love. With each breath, imagine drawing in compassion from the divine source and radiating it outward to all living beings.

Service and Acts of Kindness: Dedicate a portion of your meditation to contemplating ways in which you can serve others and show kindness. Offer a prayer asking for guidance in your compassionate actions.

Guided Meditation: Cultivating Compassion

Let's embark on a guided meditation to cultivate compassion. Find a quiet space, sit comfortably, and close your eyes. Take a few deep breaths to center yourself.

"Put on then, as God's chosen ones, holy and beloved, compassionate hearts, kindness, humility, meekness, and patience." — Colossians 3:12

Imagine yourself in a peaceful garden, surrounded by the beauty of nature. This garden represents the sanctuary of your heart, where compassion takes root and blossoms. As you walk through this garden, notice the vibrant colors of the flowers, the gentle rustling of leaves, and the soothing sound of a nearby stream.

"Let all bitterness and wrath and anger and clamor and slander be put away from you, along with all malice. Be kind to one another, tenderhearted, forgiving one another, as God in Christ forgave you." — Ephesians 4:31-32

Visualize a warm, radiant light emanating from your heart. This light symbolizes compassion—an ever-flowing source of love and empathy. With each breath, imagine this light growing brighter, expanding with compassion.

"Blessed are the merciful, for they shall receive mercy." — Matthew 5:7

Think of a specific person or group of people who may be suffering or in need of compassion. As you meditate, extend your compassion to them. Imagine sending waves of love and healing toward them, alleviating their suffering and bringing comfort.

"But love your enemies, and do good, and lend, expecting nothing in return, and your reward will be great, and you will be sons of the Most High, for he is kind to the ungrateful and the evil." — Luke 6:35

Now, expand your compassion to encompass all living beings. Visualize a world where compassion is the guiding principle, where people reach out to one another in love and understanding. Offer a prayer for a world filled with compassion.

"And above all these put on love, which binds everything together in perfect harmony." — Colossians 3:14

As you conclude this meditation, remember that compassion is not just a feeling but a way of life—a practice that calls us to action. May you carry the warmth of compassion in your heart, radiating love and empathy to all you encounter, and may you be a beacon of God's compassion in the world.

Meditation Quotes

Let these meditation quotes inspire your practice of cultivating compassion:

"Compassion is not a relationship between the healer and the wounded. It's a relationship between equals. Only when we know our own darkness well can we be present with the darkness of others." — Pema Chödrön

"Above all, keep loving one another earnestly, since love covers a multitude of sins." — 1 Peter 4:8

"If you want others to be happy, practice compassion. If you want to be happy, practice compassion." — Dalai Lama

"But the fruit of the Spirit is love, joy, peace, patience, kindness, goodness, faithfulness, gentleness, self-control; against such things there is no law." — Galatians 5:22-23

In this chapter, we have explored the sacred practice of compassion—a transformative force that binds our hearts to the divine and to one another. We have learned that compassion is more than a sentiment; it is a way of life—a practice that calls us to action. As we continue our exploration of Christian spirituality and meditation, may we embrace compassion as a guiding principle, a source of healing, and a path to a more compassionate world.

Chapter 11: Embracing the Divine Mystery

In the vast tapestry of Christian spirituality and meditation, there exists a profound dimension that transcends human comprehension—the realm of the divine mystery. It is a dimension where faith and wonder intertwine, where seekers yearn to glimpse the ineffable, and where the human spirit seeks communion with the divine. In this chapter, we will embark on a journey into the heart of the divine mystery within Christian spirituality and meditation.

We will delve into the essence of mystery, recognizing that it is not a puzzle to be solved but a presence to be encountered—a presence that elicits awe and reverence. Through the practice of meditation, we will learn how to embrace the divine mystery, opening our hearts and minds to the unfathomable depths of God's presence.

The Enigma of the Divine Mystery
    "Can you fathom the mysteries of God? Can you probe the limits of the Almighty?" — Job 11:7

The divine mystery is the enigma of God's presence—the recognition that there are aspects of the divine that transcend human understanding. It is an acknowledgment that God is beyond our grasp, beyond the confines of human language and comprehension.

In the Christian tradition, the divine mystery is deeply rooted in the belief in a God who reveals Himself while remaining veiled in mystery. It is the mystery of the Incarnation, where God became human in the person of Jesus Christ. It is the mystery of the Trinity—a triune Godhead that defies easy explanation.

The Practice of Embracing Mystery

Embracing the divine mystery through meditation is a transformative process that invites us to let go of our need for certainty and control. Here are some meditation tips to help you in this journey:

Begin with Humility: Start your meditation by acknowledging your limitations. Recognize that there are aspects of God and His plan that are beyond your comprehension. Embrace humility as a gateway to encountering the divine mystery.

Scriptural Reflection: Meditate on scriptures that invite you into the mystery of God. Isaiah 55:8-9 reminds us, "For my thoughts are not your thoughts, neither are your ways my ways, declares the Lord. For as the heavens are higher than the earth, so are my ways higher than your ways and my thoughts than your thoughts." Let these words guide your meditation.

Contemplative Silence: Practice contemplative meditation, where you sit in silence and open yourself to the presence of God. Let go of the need for words or answers and simply rest in God's presence.

Surrender of Understanding: During your meditation, surrender your need to fully understand God or His plan. Offer a prayer of surrender, trusting that God's wisdom surpasses your own.

Mystical Imagination: Use your imagination to enter into the mystery. Visualize yourself in a sacred space where the divine mystery is palpable. Allow your senses to be engaged, and simply be present in the mystery.

Guided Meditation: Embracing the Divine Mystery

Let's embark on a guided meditation to embrace the divine mystery. Find a quiet space, sit comfortably, and close your eyes. Take a few deep breaths to center yourself.

"Great is the Lord, and greatly to be praised, and his greatness is unsearchable."
— Psalm 145:3

Imagine yourself standing on the shore of an expansive, starlit ocean. The night sky is filled with constellations, each one a testament to the vastness and complexity of the universe. You stand in awe of the infinite expanse before you.

"For now we see in a mirror dimly, but then face to face. Now I know in part; then I shall know fully, even as I have been fully known." — 1 Corinthians 13:12

As you gaze at the shimmering waters, you realize that this ocean represents the divine mystery—the unfathomable depths of God's presence. You are drawn to step into the water, to immerse yourself in the mystery.

"The secret things belong to the Lord our God, but the things that are revealed belong to us and to our children forever, that we may do all the words of this law." — Deuteronomy 29:29

With each step, you feel the coolness of the water enveloping you. It is a gentle reminder that the divine mystery is not to be conquered or understood but to be experienced and embraced. As you wade further into the ocean, you sense a profound peace and a deepening connection with God.

"Be still, and know that I am God. I will be exalted among the nations, I will be exalted in the earth!" — Psalm 46:10

As you conclude this meditation, remember that embracing the divine mystery is a lifelong journey—a journey of faith, wonder, and reverence. May you continue to be drawn into the depths of God's presence, where certainty gives way to awe, and understanding gives way to wonder.

Meditation Quotes

Let these meditation quotes inspire your practice of embracing the divine mystery:

"The most beautiful experience we can have is the mysterious. It is the fundamental emotion that stands at the cradle of true art and true science." — Albert Einstein

"O the depth of the riches and wisdom and knowledge of God! How unsearchable are his judgments and how inscrutable his ways!" — Romans 11:33

"The soul loves the mystery, for it knows that the mystery is where all transformation takes place." — John O'Donohue

"Seek the Lord and his strength; seek his presence continually!" — 1 Chronicles 16:11

In this chapter, we have embarked on a journey into the heart of the divine mystery within Christian spirituality and meditation. We have learned that the divine mystery is not a puzzle to be solved but a presence to be encountered—a presence that elicits awe and reverence. As we continue our exploration, may we embrace the divine mystery with humility, wonder, and a deepening faith that leads us into the unfathomable depths of God's presence.

Chapter 12: The Sacred Path of Surrender

In the tapestry of Christian spirituality and meditation, surrender is the golden thread that weaves our individual journeys into the divine masterpiece of God's plan. It is a profound act of trust—a letting go of our own desires, control, and ego, and an embrace of God's will with an open heart. In this chapter, we will explore the sacred path of surrender within the context of Christian spirituality and meditation.

We will delve into the essence of surrender, understanding that it is not a passive resignation but an active response—an act of love and devotion to God. Through the practice of meditation, we will learn how to cultivate surrender as a way of life, a way that leads us to a deeper connection with God and a richer experience of His grace.

The Essence of Surrender

"I have been crucified with Christ. It is no longer I who live, but Christ who lives in me. And the life I now live in the flesh I live by faith in the Son of God, who loved me and gave himself for me." — Galatians 2:20

Surrender is the act of yielding our will to the divine will—an act of self-emptying, where our ego and desires are crucified with Christ. It is an acknowledgment that God's wisdom surpasses our own, and His plan is greater than our understanding.

In the Christian tradition, surrender is deeply intertwined with the life and teachings of Jesus Christ. He exemplified surrender in the Garden of Gethsemane when He prayed, "Not my will, but yours be done." It is a surrender to God's love, mercy, and divine providence.

The Practice of Surrender

Cultivating surrender through meditation is a transformative process that requires a willingness to let go of our attachments and control. Here are some meditation tips to help you in this journey:

Begin with Relinquishment: Start your meditation by consciously letting go of your worries, fears, and desires. Release them into God's hands, acknowledging that He is in control.

Scriptural Reflection: Meditate on scriptures that emphasize surrender. Proverbs 3:5-6 reminds us, "Trust in the Lord with all your heart, and do not lean on your own understanding. In all your ways acknowledge him, and he will make straight your paths." Let these words guide your meditation.

Breath of Surrender: During your meditation, focus on your breath as a symbol of surrender. As you inhale, imagine drawing in God's presence and His will. As you exhale, release your own desires and ego.

Centering Prayer: Practice centering prayer, a form of Christian meditation where you sit in silent contemplation, allowing thoughts to pass without attachment. Simply rest in God's presence and surrender to His love.

Prayer of Surrender: Dedicate a portion of your meditation to offering a prayer of surrender. Express your willingness to follow God's will and invite His guidance in your life.

Guided Meditation: The Sacred Path of Surrender

Let's embark on a guided meditation to explore the sacred path of surrender. Find a quiet space, sit comfortably, and close your eyes. Take a few deep breaths to center yourself.

"Not my will, but yours be done." — Luke 22:42

Imagine yourself in a serene garden, bathed in a soft, golden light. This garden represents the sanctuary of surrender, where the ego and desires yield to God's loving presence. As you walk through this garden, notice the beauty of each flower, the vibrant colors, and the gentle rustling of leaves.

"I appeal to you therefore, brothers, by the mercies of God, to present your bodies as a living sacrifice, holy and acceptable to God, which is your spiritual worship." — Romans 12:1

Visualize a radiant, loving presence before you. This presence is God—the source of all love, wisdom, and grace. As you stand before God, offer Him your heart, your will, and your life. Express your willingness to surrender all that you are.

"Take my yoke upon you, and learn from me, for I am gentle and lowly in heart, and you will find rest for your souls." — Matthew 11:29

Feel God's loving embrace as He accepts your surrender. Sense the burdens of your ego and desires being lifted from your shoulders. Experience a profound sense of peace and rest in His presence.

"And he said to all, 'If anyone would come after me, let him deny himself and take up his cross daily and follow me.'" — Luke 9:23

As you conclude this meditation, remember that surrender is not a one-time event but an ongoing journey—a journey of trust, love, and devotion to God. May you continue to walk the sacred path of surrender, yielding your will to God's divine plan, and may you find the freedom and grace that come with letting go.

Meditation Quotes

Let these meditation quotes inspire your practice of embracing the sacred path of surrender:

"Surrender to God is the most difficult yet most important act of our will. It opens our hearts to His transformative grace." — Unknown

"For whoever would save his life will lose it, but whoever loses his life for my sake will find it." — Matthew 16:25

"Surrender means the decision to stop fighting the world and to start loving it." — Richard Rohr

"Therefore I tell you, whatever you ask in prayer, believe that you have received it, and it will be yours." — Mark 11:24

In this chapter, we have embarked on a journey into the heart of surrender within Christian spirituality and meditation. We have learned that surrender is not a passive resignation but an active response—an act of love and devotion to God. As we continue our exploration, may we embrace the sacred path of surrender with humility, trust, and a deepening faith that leads us into the loving embrace of our   Creator.

Chapter 13: The Divine Dance of Silence

In the intricate tapestry of Christian spirituality and meditation, there exists a profound symphony of silence—an ever-present undercurrent that carries the whispers of the divine. It is within the sanctuary of silence that we encounter God in the most intimate and profound ways. In this chapter, we will explore the divine dance of silence within Christian spirituality and meditation.

We will delve into the essence of silence, understanding that it is not merely the absence of noise but a sacred space—an invitation to stillness, contemplation, and communion with God. Through the practice of meditation, we will learn how to embrace the divine dance of silence, opening our hearts to the transformative power of quietude and inner peace.

The Essence of Silence

"The Lord is in his holy temple; let all the earth keep silence before him." — Habakkuk 2:20

Silence is the language of the soul—a space where words are inadequate, and the presence of God is felt in the depths of our being. It is an acknowledgment that God often speaks in whispers, inviting us to listen with the ears of the heart.

In the Christian tradition, silence holds a revered place as a means of encountering the divine. It is a way to step away from the noise and distractions of the world and draw near to God's presence. It is in silence that we create the space for God to speak to us and for us to respond in the language of the soul.

The Practice of Silence

Cultivating the divine dance of silence through meditation is a transformative process that requires a willingness to let go of external distractions and enter into the inner sanctuary of the heart. Here are some meditation tips to help you in this journey:

Begin with Stillness: Start your meditation by finding a quiet and comfortable space. Sit in a relaxed posture, close your eyes, and take a few deep breaths to settle into stillness.

Scriptural Reflection: Meditate on scriptures that highlight the importance of silence. Psalm 46:10 encourages us, "Be still, and know that I am God." Let these words guide your meditation.

Centering Prayer: Practice centering prayer, a form of Christian meditation that emphasizes silence and presence. Choose a sacred word or phrase to gently return to whenever your mind wanders.

Breath Awareness: Focus on your breath as a way to anchor yourself in the present moment. As you breathe in and out, let go of thoughts and distractions, returning to the rhythm of your breath.

Listening in Silence: Dedicate a portion of your meditation to simply listening in silence. Invite God's presence and be receptive to any insights, guidance, or peace that may arise.

Guided Meditation: The Divine Dance of Silence
    Let's embark on a guided meditation to experience the divine dance of silence. Find a quiet space, sit comfortably, and close your eyes. Take a few deep breaths to center yourself.

"Be still, and know that I am God." — Psalm 46:10

Imagine yourself in a sacred chapel or a serene natural setting. You are surrounded by a profound hush—a silence that seems to embrace you like a gentle breeze. As you sit in this space of quietude, you sense the presence of God drawing near.

"In the beginning was the Word, and the Word was with God, and the Word was God." — John 1:1

In this silence, you begin to realize that God often speaks in the language of silence—the Word before words. It is a language that transcends human language and touches the deepest recesses of the heart.

"But the Lord is in his holy temple; let all the earth keep silence before him." — Habakkuk 2:20

As you listen in silence, you become aware of the symphony of creation—the rustling leaves, the chirping birds, the gentle flow of a stream. Each sound seems to harmonize with the silence, creating a sacred music of the soul.

"For God alone, O my soul, wait in silence, for my hope is from him." — Psalm 62:5

Now, turn your attention inward. Within the depths of your being, you encounter a profound stillness—a sanctuary where your soul meets God's presence. In this inner silence, offer your prayers, your hopes, your fears, and your gratitude.

"In returning and rest you shall be saved; in quietness and in trust shall be your strength." — Isaiah 30:15

As you conclude this meditation, remember that the divine dance of silence is not an escape from the world but a return to the source of all life and meaning. May you carry the peace and presence of silence into your daily life, listening for God's whispers amid the noise of the world.

Meditation Quotes

Let these meditation quotes inspire your practice of embracing the divine dance of silence:

"Silence is the language of God; all else is poor translation." — Rumi

"But the Lord is in his holy temple; let all the earth keep silence before him." —
Habakkuk 2:20

"In the silence of the heart, God speaks." — Mother Teresa

"The words of the wise heard in quiet are better than the shouting of a ruler among fools." — Ecclesiastes 9:17

In this chapter, we have explored the profound dimension of the divine dance of silence within Christian spirituality and meditation. We have learned that silence is not merely the absence of noise but a sacred space—an invitation to stillness, contemplation, and communion with God. As we continue our exploration, may we embrace the divine dance of silence with reverence, openness, and a willingness to listen to the whispers of the divine in the depths of our hearts.

Chapter 14: The Journey Within: Exploring the Inner Sanctum

In the intricate tapestry of Christian spirituality and meditation, the journey within is a sacred pilgrimage—a path that leads us to the inner sanctum of the soul, where we encounter the divine presence. It is a profound exploration of our inner landscape, a journey into the depths of our being where God's Spirit dwells. In this chapter, we will embark on this transformative journey within Christian spirituality and meditation.

We will delve into the essence of the inner journey, understanding that it is not a mere self-discovery but a quest for deeper communion with God. Through the practice of meditation, we will learn how to navigate the inner terrain, opening our hearts to the transformative power of self-awareness, inner healing, and divine encounter.

The Essence of the Inner Journey

"The kingdom of God is within you." — Luke 17:21

The inner journey is an exploration of the kingdom of God within—the recognition that the divine presence resides within the depths of our souls. It is an acknowledgment that we are fearfully and wonderfully made, each of us a sacred vessel capable of hosting God's presence.

In the Christian tradition, the inner journey is deeply rooted in the teachings of Jesus Christ. He invited His disciples to seek the kingdom of God within and to abide in Him as branches on the vine. It is a journey of self-discovery in the context of divine relationship.

The Practice of the Inner Journey

Cultivating the inner journey through meditation is a transformative process that requires self-awareness, self-compassion, and a willingness to confront the shadows within us. Here are some meditation tips to help you in this journey:

Begin with Self-Awareness: Start your meditation by turning your attention inward. Reflect on your thoughts, emotions, and inner state. Acknowledge any areas of tension, pain, or longing within you.

Scriptural Reflection: Meditate on scriptures that guide you in the inner journey. Psalm 139:23-24 encourages us, "Search me, O God, and know my heart! Try me and know my thoughts! And see if there be any grievous way in me, and lead me in the way everlasting." Let these words guide your meditation.

Inner Healing Meditation: Dedicate a portion of your meditation to inner healing. Visualize God's healing light penetrating the areas of woundedness or brokenness within you. Surrender these areas to God for healing and restoration.

Contemplative Silence: Practice contemplative meditation, where you sit in silence and simply observe your inner thoughts and feelings without judgment. Allow God's presence to permeate your inner world.

Divine Encounter: In your meditation, seek a deep encounter with God's presence within you. Invite Him to speak to your heart, to reveal His love and guidance, and to lead you in the way of truth.

Guided Meditation: The Journey Within

Let's embark on a guided meditation to explore the inner sanctum of the soul. Find a quiet space, sit comfortably, and close your eyes. Take a few deep breaths to center yourself.

"Search me, O God, and know my heart! Try me and know my thoughts!" — Psalm 139:23

Imagine yourself standing at the threshold of a sacred temple—a temple that represents your inner world. The entrance is adorned with intricate carvings and symbols, each holding a deeper meaning. As you step inside, you enter the sanctuary of your soul.

"The Spirit himself bears witness with our spirit that we are children of God." — Romans 8:16

Within this sanctuary, you are met with a profound stillness—a hallowed silence that envelops you like a loving embrace. You sense the presence of God's Spirit dwelling here, ready to guide you on your inner journey.

"Create in me a clean heart, O God, and renew a right spirit within me." — Psalm 51:10

Take a moment to reflect on your inner state. Are there areas of your heart that need healing, forgiveness, or transformation? As you identify these areas, visualize them as doors within the temple.

"I will give you a new heart, and a new spirit I will put within you." — Ezekiel 36:26

Choose one of these doors to explore in this meditation. As you open it, you may encounter memories, emotions, or wounds. Invite God's healing presence to enter with you. Experience His love and grace bringing healing and restoration.

"And he who searches hearts knows what is the mind of the Spirit, because the Spirit intercedes for the saints according to the will of God." — Romans 8:27

As you conclude this meditation, remember that the journey within is an ongoing exploration—a journey of self-awareness, inner healing, and divine encounter. May you continue to delve into the depths of your soul, encountering God's presence and experiencing transformation.

Meditation Quotes

Let these meditation quotes inspire your practice of the inner journey:

"The closer you come to knowing that you alone create the world of your experience, the more vital it becomes for you to discover just who is doing the creating." — Eric Micha'el Leventhal

"Create in me a clean heart, O God, and renew a right spirit within me." — Psalm 51:10

"Be still and know that I am God." — Psalm 46:10

"The greatest journey one can take is the journey within." — Unknown

In this chapter, we have embarked on a transformative journey into the inner sanctum of the soul within Christian spirituality and meditation. We have learned that the inner journey is a sacred pilgrimage—a path that leads us to the depths of our being, where we encounter the divine presence. As we continue our exploration, may we embrace the journey within with self-awareness, self-compassion, and a deepening connection with God's Spirit, experiencing transformation and spiritual growth.

Chapter 15: The Sacred Union: Communion with God

In the final chapter of our journey through Christian spirituality and meditation, we arrive at a profound moment—a moment of sacred union, where the human soul and the divine Spirit embrace in communion. It is the culmination of our exploration, the fulfillment of our longing, and the realization of our deepest desire—to be one with God. In this chapter, we will delve into the experience of communion with God within Christian spirituality and meditation.

We will explore the essence of communion, understanding that it is not a distant hope but a present reality—a reality that invites us to partake in the divine life. Through the practice of meditation, we will learn how to enter into the sacred union, opening our hearts to the transformative power of divine love, intimacy, and oneness.

The Essence of Communion

"Abide in me, and I in you. As the branch cannot bear fruit by itself, unless it abides in the vine, neither can you, unless you abide in me." — John 15:4

Communion is the embrace of love—a union where the soul abides in God and God in the soul. It is an acknowledgment that we are called to be branches connected to the divine vine, drawing life, nourishment, and purpose from our union with God.

In the Christian tradition, communion is central to the faith. It is celebrated in the Eucharist, where bread and wine become the body and blood of Christ. It is a reminder that through Christ, we enter into a sacred union with God, a union that nourishes and sustains our spiritual journey.

The Practice of Communion

Cultivating communion with God through meditation is a transformative process that requires surrender, receptivity, and a longing for intimacy. Here are some meditation tips to help you in this journey:

Begin with Longing: Start your meditation with a deep longing to be in communion with God. Let your heart's desire for intimacy be the catalyst for your practice.

Scriptural Reflection: Meditate on scriptures that speak of communion with God. 1 Corinthians 6:17 reminds us, "But he who is joined to the Lord becomes one spirit with him." Let these words guide your meditation.

Eucharistic Meditation: Visualize the Eucharist during your meditation. Imagine partaking in the body and blood of Christ and feel the union with Him. Allow this visualization to deepen your sense of communion.

Heart-Centered Prayer: Practice heart-centered prayer, where you focus on your heart as the center of your communion with God. Imagine your heart as a sacred chamber where God's presence resides.

Listening in Stillness: Dedicate a portion of your meditation to simply listening to God's voice. In the silence, allow Him to speak to your heart, to reveal His love, and to draw you closer into union.

Guided Meditation: The Sacred Union

Let's embark on a guided meditation to experience the sacred union with God. Find a quiet space, sit comfortably, and close your eyes. Take a few deep breaths to center yourself.

"Abide in me, and I in you." — John 15:4

Imagine yourself in a place of profound stillness—a sanctuary of communion with God. You are enveloped in a warm, golden light that radiates love and grace. As you sit in this sacred space, you sense the presence of God drawing near.

"I am the vine; you are the branches. Whoever abides in me and I in him, he it is that bears much fruit." — John 15:5

Visualize yourself as a branch connected to a magnificent vine—the vine of Christ. Feel the life-giving sap of His presence flowing through you, nourishing your soul, and filling you with His love.

"For in him we live and move and have our being." — Acts 17:28

In this union, you realize that you are not separate from God but intimately connected to Him. You are one spirit with Him, and His love flows through every fiber of your being. Experience the profound sense of oneness and intimacy.

"He who eats my flesh and drinks my blood abides in me, and I in him." — John 6:56

As you conclude this meditation, remember that communion with God is not a distant goal but a present reality. It is a union that sustains and nourishes your spiritual journey, a union that offers love, grace, and intimacy beyond measure.

Meditation Quotes

Let these meditation quotes inspire your practice of communion with God:

"The soul that is in union with God is the soul that is truly alive." — Unknown

"I have been crucified with Christ. It is no longer I who live, but Christ who lives in me." — Galatians 2:20

"In him we live and move and have our being." — Acts 17:28

"Draw near to God, and he will draw near to you." — James 4:8

In this final chapter, we have reached the culmination of our journey—the experience of communion with God within Christian spirituality and meditation. We have learned that communion is not a distant hope but a present reality, a union that offers love, grace, and intimacy beyond measure. As we conclude our exploration, may we continue to cultivate communion with God, abiding in His love, and living out our divine union in the world.

Chapter 16: The Journey Continues: Living the Meditative Life

As we approach the conclusion of our exploration of Christian spirituality and meditation, we find ourselves at a pivotal moment—a moment of transition and continuation. Our journey does not end with the final chapter but rather enters a new phase—a phase where the insights, practices, and experiences of meditation become woven into the fabric of our daily lives. In this chapter, we will delve into the art of living the meditative life within Christian spirituality.

We will explore the essence of a meditative life, understanding that it is not confined to a cushion or a quiet corner but extends to every aspect of our existence. Through the practice of meditation, we have laid the foundation, and now, we will learn how to carry the transformative power of meditation into our relationships, actions, and responses to life's challenges.

The Essence of a Meditative Life

"But be doers of the word, and not hearers only, deceiving yourselves." — James 1:22

A meditative life is a life of integration—a life where the insights gained in moments of stillness and contemplation find expression in our everyday actions and interactions. It is an acknowledgment that meditation is not an isolated practice but a way of being, a way of living out our faith in practical, tangible ways.

In the Christian tradition, a meditative life aligns with the teachings of Jesus Christ, who called His disciples to be salt and light in the world. It is a life that radiates the love, compassion, and wisdom of Christ to all we encounter.

The Practice of a Meditative Life

Living a meditative life is a transformative process that requires mindfulness, intentionality, and a commitment to embodying our faith. Here are some practical tips to help you in this journey:

Begin with Awareness: Start your day with a moment of awareness. Before the rush of activities, take a few deep breaths and set an intention to carry the presence of God with you throughout the day.

Scriptural Reflection: Choose a scripture or a verse that resonates with you, and carry it with you as a reminder throughout the day. Let it guide your thoughts and actions.

Mindful Presence: Practice mindfulness in everyday tasks. Whether you're eating, walking, or working, be fully present in the moment, acknowledging God's presence in the ordinary.

Loving-Kindness: Cultivate a heart of loving-kindness. Offer blessings and prayers for those you encounter, even in challenging situations. Remember Christ's teaching to love your neighbor.

Grace-Filled Responses: When faced with difficulties or conflicts, pause and breathe before responding. Ask for the guidance of the Holy Spirit to respond with love, grace, and wisdom.

Guided Meditation: Living the Meditative Life

Let's embark on a guided meditation to explore the art of living the meditative life. Find a quiet space, sit comfortably, and close your eyes. Take a few deep breaths to center yourself.

"Let your light shine before others, so that they may see your good works and give glory to your Father who is in heaven." — Matthew 5:16

Imagine yourself standing at the threshold of a new day—a day filled with opportunities to embody the love and wisdom you have cultivated through meditation. Visualize a radiant light within your heart, representing the presence of God.

"Whatever you do, in word or deed, do everything in the name of the Lord Jesus, giving thanks to God the Father through him." — Colossians 3:17

As you go about your day, see this inner light shining through your thoughts, words, and actions. Whether you're interacting with family, friends, colleagues, or strangers, let this light be a source of love, compassion, and grace.

"Love your neighbor as yourself." — Mark 12:31

In moments of challenge or conflict, pause and return to your inner light. Breathe deeply, and invite God's presence to guide your response. Seek understanding, forgiveness, and reconciliation, reflecting Christ's love.

"Therefore be imitators of God, as beloved children. And walk in love, as Christ loved us and gave himself up for us." — Ephesians 5:1-2

As you conclude this meditation, remember that living the meditative life is an ongoing journey—a journey of mindful presence, loving-kindness, and grace-filled responses. May you continue to carry the transformative power of meditation into every aspect of your life, becoming a beacon of light and love in the world.

Meditation Quotes

Let these meditation quotes inspire your practice of living the meditative life:

"Let your light shine before others, so that they may see your good works and give glory to your Father who is in heaven." — Matthew 5:16

"Whatever you do, in word or deed, do everything in the name of the Lord Jesus, giving thanks to God the Father through him." — Colossians 3:17

"And walk in love, as Christ loved us and gave himself up for us." — Ephesians 5:1-2

"The goal of meditation is not to control your thoughts, but to stop letting them control you." — Unknown

In this final chapter, we have arrived at a new beginning—a beginning of living the meditative life within Christian spirituality and meditation. We have learned that a meditative life is a life of integration and embodiment, a life that radiates the love, compassion, and wisdom of Christ in practical, tangible ways. As we conclude our journey, may we continue to walk this path of mindful presence and loving-kindness, becoming living expressions of God's grace and love in the world.

Conclusion

As we draw the final curtain on our profound journey through the realms of Christian spirituality and meditation, it is with hearts filled with gratitude, reverence, and hope that we reflect upon the tapestry we have woven. The chapters we have traversed, the scriptures we have contemplated, and the meditative practices we have embraced have led us to a deeper understanding of ourselves, our faith, and our divine connection.

In this concluding chapter, we stand at the threshold of a new beginning—a beginning that encapsulates the essence of our exploration, a beginning that invites us to take the insights gained and weave them into the very fabric of our lives. It is a beginning that beckons us to become living testaments to the transformative power of Christian meditation.

Embracing the Wisdom of Meditation

"But the wisdom from above is first pure, then peaceable, gentle, open to reason, full of mercy and good fruits, impartial and sincere." — James 3:17

Throughout our journey, we have unearthed the wisdom that flows from the sacred practice of meditation. We have discovered that meditation is not a passive exercise but a dynamic engagement with the divine. It is a journey inward—a journey to the heart of our faith, where we encounter God's presence in profound ways.

In our pursuit of wisdom, we have learned that meditation is a path to purity of heart, a source of peace in turbulent times, a wellspring of gentleness, and a harbor of reason and discernment. It is a channel through which we receive the gifts of mercy, bear the fruits of goodness, impartiality, and sincerity—a wisdom that aligns our hearts with the divine heart.

Embracing the Beauty of Scripture

"Your word is a lamp to my feet and a light to my path." — Psalm 119:105

Throughout our journey, the scriptures have been our faithful companions— guiding, illuminating, and revealing the timeless truths that anchor our faith. The Word of God has been a lamp to our feet and a light to our path, leading us through the shadows of doubt and confusion.

In our quest to embrace the beauty of scripture, we have discovered that it is not merely ink on parchment but a living word—an ever-present, ever-relevant source of inspiration and guidance. We have learned to listen deeply to the scriptures, to savor their nuances, and to allow them to permeate our hearts, transforming our lives from the inside out.

Embracing the Power of Meditation

"Be still, and know that I am God." — Psalm 46:10

Meditation, as we have come to understand, is not a passive endeavor but an active surrender—a surrender of our restless minds and anxious hearts to the divine presence. It is an invitation to be still, to cultivate the sacred art of listening, and to know that God is indeed with us.

In our exploration of meditation, we have unearthed its transformative power—a power that quiets the storms within us, that heals the wounds of our souls, and that opens the door to encounters with the divine. We have learned that meditation is a journey within, a journey to the inner sanctum of the soul, where we commune with the Creator of all.

Embracing the Journey Within

"The kingdom of God is within you." — Luke 17:21

Our journey within, we have discovered, is the most sacred pilgrimage of all. It is a journey to the heart of our faith, where we encounter the kingdom of God within us. It is an acknowledgment that we are fearfully and wonderfully made—each of us a sacred vessel capable of hosting God's presence.

In our exploration of the journey within, we have delved into the essence of the inner journey, recognizing that it is not a mere self-discovery but a quest for deeper communion with God. Through the practice of meditation, we have learned to navigate the inner terrain, opening our hearts to the transformative power of self-awareness, inner healing, and divine encounter.

Embracing the Sacred Union

"Abide in me, and I in you." — John 15:4

In our final chapter, we experienced the sacred union—the moment of communion with God that is the culmination of our journey. We learned that communion is not a distant hope but a present reality—a reality that invites us to partake in the divine life. We discovered that communion is the embrace of love—a union where the soul abides in God and God in the soul.

In our guided meditation, we visualized ourselves as branches connected to the vine of Christ, experiencing the profound sense of oneness and intimacy. We realized that we are not separate from God but intimately connected to Him, one spirit with Him, and that this communion sustains and nourishes our spiritual journey.

Embracing the Meditative Life

Our journey does not end here; rather, it enters a new phase—a phase where the insights, practices, and experiences of meditation become woven into the fabric of our daily lives. We have explored the essence of a meditative life, understanding that it is not confined to a cushion or a quiet corner but extends to every aspect of our existence.

We have learned to begin each day with awareness, to carry scriptures in our hearts, to practice mindful presence in everyday tasks, to cultivate loving-kindness, and to respond to life's challenges with grace and wisdom. We have become living expressions of God's grace and love in the world—a beacon of light.

The Journey Continues

As we conclude our exploration of Christian spirituality and meditation, let us remember that the journey continues—a journey of deepening faith, ongoing meditation, and a life lived in alignment with divine wisdom and love. Let us carry the transformative power of meditation into every aspect of our lives, becoming living testaments to the beauty and depth of our faith.

May the wisdom, beauty, and power of Christian spirituality and meditation continue to guide you on your sacred journey—a journey of spiritual growth, divine communion, and lasting inner peace. Embrace the tapestry of faith and meditation, and may it be a source of inspiration and transformation for all who seek the path of the heart.

In closing, let us reflect on the words of the psalmist:

"I will meditate on your precepts and fix my eyes on your ways." — Psalm 119:15

May we, too, meditate on God's precepts and fix our eyes on His ways, for in this sacred practice, we find the essence of Christian spirituality—the profound and timeless journey of the heart.

Bethel Eneojo

Printed in Great Britain
by Amazon